Personal Growth and Development

REIKI
FOR
BEGINNERS

MONIQUE JOINER SIEDLAK

Oshun
Publications

Cover Design by MJS

Cover Image by Vadmary@depositphotos.com

Published by Oshun Publications

www.oshunpublications.com

Contents

Other Books in the Series

Want to learn about African Magic, Wicca, or even Reiki while cleaning your home, exercising, or driving to work? I know it's tough these days to simply find the time to relax and curl up with a good book. This is why I'm delighted to share that I have books available in audiobook format.

Best of all, you can get the audiobook version of this book or any other book by me for free as part of a 30-day Audible trial.

Members get free audiobooks every month and exclusive discounts. It's an excellent way to explore and determine if audiobook learning works for you.

If you're not satisfied, you can cancel anytime within the

trial period. You won't be charged, and you can still keep your book. To choose your free audiobook, visit:

www.mojosiedlak.com/free-audiobooks

WANT TO BE FIRST TO KNOW?!

JOIN MY NEWSLETTER!
MOJOSIEDLAK.COM/SELF-HELP-AND-YOGA-NEWSLETTER

Introduction

Sometimes things happen in life that will completely drain your energy, and usually without warning. Feelings of negativity overwhelm your mind, and your body will start to react through pain or fatigue. Even your posture becomes slumped from constant stress. This is your sign that you need to take back control of your life.

Positivity is a state of mind, but sometimes you need help to regain optimism. Luckily, Reiki can assist you in this journey. Originating in Japan, Reiki is a method for reducing stress, encouraging healing, and improving relaxation feelings. Reiki considers both the spirit and energy, which encompasses a full life. Ki (or more popularly known as Chi) is a life force energy within the body and manifests itself physically and mentally. Reiki strengthens Ki forces and promotes the proper flow of Ki.

Reiki requires spirituality. It is not a specific religion, but the energy from treatments often strengthens religious bonds that a person may hold. Regardless, Reiki focuses on internal energy sources and works even in the absence of religious doctrines. Reiki encourages harmonious living, as exemplified by founder Mikao Usui. Harmony, peace, and ethical decision-making should be present for natural healing to take full effect.

Reiki treatments leave you feeling radiant and more positive. The hands are the power center for Reiki. They are the passageway to healing and allow positive energy to flow throughout the body. This method is safe; it does not require expensive equipment and has many benefits. You can use Reiki alone or as a supplement to medical therapy. Many people add Reiki meditations as a way to better focus their attention on healing energy.

Reiki has an inextricable link to the body. Specifically, the seven chakras, which act as energy vortexes that align with the endocrine system. Each chakra has a location along a vertical line in the body that powers certain emotions and can heal specific body areas. Similarly, the endocrine system releases hormones that regulate your system. This relationship between Reiki and the physical body is undeniable. Learning Reiki opens the communication channels between the physical body and spiritual energy. It helps your body heal itself through two methods, which hastens restoration while stimulating positivity.

Anybody can learn Reiki techniques. It is not a challenging feat that takes a lifetime to discover, nor do you need a degree to practice Reiki. Traditionally, a person learns Reiki through knowledge transfer when attending a training session. During these sessions, a Reiki Master transfers positive energy to you by the 'laying on of hands.' You use these lessons and hand positions to treat yourself and others. This book assists in the teachings of Reiki so you can heal from the inside and exude positivity.

Reiki training is accessible, but you must be willing to learn and believe in the work. There are three degrees of Reiki, and each level will bring you closer to the universal energy source. Increasing your knowledge and getting hands-on practice is the best way to become a Reiki Master. Some of the things you will learn include the healing hands positions, meditation techniques, and how to unlock energy sources.

Do you want to heal yourself naturally? Do you want to improve your energy levels? Reiki is the way; let's get started!

ONE

Benefits of Reiki Healing

REIKI HAS MANY EMOTIONAL AND PHYSICAL BENEFITS. IT alleviates pain, improves sleep quality, and reduces stress levels. Many individuals have been known to experience less anxiety and fewer depressive episodes after attending Reiki treatments. Stress, illness, and injury can harm your body. Still, the gentle touch of Reiki reverses this damage positively and energetically.

Restores Balance

Balance and harmony are important in Reiki. An energy transfer assists your body in improving total wellness. Using only your hands means that Reiki does not require confusing or intricate procedures. It does not strain the body like an exercise, which means people of all physical levels can be open to Reiki treatments. Reiki focuses on your spirit, body, and mind, so your entire body equalizes its systems, and positive energy balances out any negativity. This balance is a constant reminder to stay in the moment. Your focus remains on the present situation rather than becoming anxious over things that are out of your control. Positive energy creates channels of acceptance and makes you more amenable to tense situations.

Reduces Stress and Tension

Reiki relaxes the body and brings peace to the mind. During treatment, a person enjoys energy input, which makes them more receptive to positive attitudes. You do not have to enable emotional walls or put on a brave face. You can simply be yourself. This mindset clears your mind and removes tension from your body. Stress levels become lower, and you can focus on being the best version of yourself. After the laying of hands, it is common to experience a sense of euphoria and enlightened optimism. A positive attitude becomes prevalent, and people feel at peace with themselves.

Cleanses and Strengthens

Bad eating habits, busy lives, and insufficient sleep damage our bodies. Your immune system becomes weaker, and your body fights hard to rid itself of impurities. Sometimes, our bodies do not have enough strength or are not given sufficient resting time to repair itself. Yet, Reiki forces you to relax through energy distribution throughout the body. This relaxation and open mindset give your body the strength to fix itself. Reiki reminds the brain and other organs that they have to repair the body. This reminder starts a detoxification process that eliminates impurities and heals your body. Reiki strengthens your immune system, decreases the chances of burnout, and acts as protective energy.

Increases Energy Flow and Productivity

Negative emotions are abundant in our daily lives. Fear, irrational thoughts, pain, anger, and mood swings take over your mind and create obstacles. Luckily, Reiki removes these negative emotions and replaces them with stronger positive ones. Regular Reiki sessions remove mental and physical energy blockers, which improves energy circulation. Increasing energy flow improves mental capacity, enables learning, allows you to think logically, and manages stress levels. Reiki can make you more productive by releasing more energy into the body.

Decreases Insomnia

Many people struggle to sleep at night. Daily tensions, troublesome finances, and other problems cause them to lie awake at night. Sleeping too few hours and waking up regularly does not allow your body to get the rest it needs. You may find you feel tired and agitated quickly. Reiki calms down these feelings and eases the body. Some individuals find Reiki so soothing that they fall asleep during treatment. This soothing remains with you for an extended period, so you can get more restful, uninterrupted sleep. Some patients will tune into past Reiki sessions when they are getting ready for bed. Recalling this time and its positive connotations can calm your mind. This optimistic outlook improves sleep patterns through deep breathing, and upon waking, you will notice a lightness in your step.

Helps with Addiction

Reiki has many benefits for those struggling with addiction or rehab. It can help those reliant on drugs or alcohol to manage cravings and makes withdrawal tolerable. Reiki relaxes the person and makes them feel in control of their decisions because they can think more logically. This calm demeanor is essential during the first phases of recovery. The harmony and balance achieved through Reiki give individuals something to look forward to in the future. Reiki alleviates feelings of resentment or anger that a recovering addict may have towards themselves in difficult or negative situations. Addicts often struggle with their self-esteem, but the positivity that Reiki instills can manage these emotions.

Provides Perspective

Emotional imbalances cause unpredictable behavior and generally make a person feel unwell. The harmonious and uplifting nature of Reiki allows you to find an emotional balance. Even when everything else seems a mess, a Reiki session gives you a chance to reflect and see the goodness in every situation. Your outlook on life improves, and positivity flows outward through your emotions. It enhances your mood because you start to consider more than just your current point of view.

Complements Traditional Medicine

Some doctors recommend Reiki sessions in addition to surgery or to manage medical conditions. Studies have shown that patients receiving Reiki treatments before and after surgery experienced less pain, increased stable vital signs, and were less anxious. These physical manifestations, combined with an enhanced mood, allowed patients to recover faster after an invasive procedure. Reiki is also beneficial for individuals undergoing long-term treatments, such as chemotherapy for cancer. Frequent Reiki sessions help these patients to manage their anxiety and maintain positivity during difficult times. A clear, calm mind enables patients to focus on recovery and manage pain without taking additional medications.

Heals the Entire Body

Reiki focuses on internal balancing through external sources of energy. A Reiki session is a reflection opportunity that pleases the mind, body, and soul. Your internal systems slow down and realign with near-normal biological rhythms. Besides developing mental strength and resilience, Reiki improves blood pressure, heart rate, and circulation. You also pay attention to your breathing, so all your organs get more oxygen. Reiki is an all-around enhancer, and these collaborative benefits allow you to heal from the inside-out. Individuals with chronic pain often use Reiki for full-body healing. A chronic condition frequently creates depression, but Reiki creates a positive mindset. People can use it to manage their daily expectations and pain.

Encourages Altruistic Emotions

Reiki is a selfless act. Many people who discover the benefits of Reiki want to make a difference in the lives of other people. Individuals who undergo Reiki sessions may feel they can face the world's challenges more easily. They realize that Reiki plays a large role in their own life and wants to share this joy with friends and family. Some people even pursue Reiki in their spare time to provide treatment to those in need. The ability to help others gives feelings of elation, which can promote harmony within a small community. You do not have to provide Reiki treatments to people on a full-time basis. Even one session a week will bring joy, but remember to first take care of your mental and emotional health.

TWO

Reiki Principles

REIKI ENERGY IS AVAILABLE TO EVERYBODY. IT IS AN IDEOLOGY
that goes a lot further than just a physical treatment session.
Mikao Usui focuses attention on five principles that are the
basis for Reiki. These principles are the cornerstone beliefs for
all Reiki practitioners, but everyday people can use these principles. The Reiki principles are guidelines for living.
Embodying these principles on a daily basis creates positive
energy and mindfulness. All of the principles focus on "just for
today" so you can stay in the moment. Maintaining a positive
disposition is difficult, but these principles make it easier to
take today one step at a time.

Just for Today, I Will Not Worry

Stress is a constant companion for most people. We are
constantly worrying about a thousand little things. Most of
them are out of our control, and the rest will likely sort themselves out. Yet, we fret over every little detail. Worrying less
decreases your stress levels and gives you a peaceful demeanor.
Your calm presence can affect others and make the world

more harmonious. Take it one day at a time and make reducing worry your next challenge. If a bad day is proving to be too difficult, stop focusing on the issues for the next hour. You will notice after a while that your anxiety has decreased, and you feel happier.

Anxiety is a natural stress response, but you need to control it. Constant worrying is bad for your physical and mental health. Take a moment to pause between your anxious thoughts. Why are you worried? Try to pinpoint the exact reason for these feelings. If you cannot control the outcome of events, then let it go. If you can make a difference or change the events' result, then take decisive action to decrease your stress. And always remember to breathe.

Just for Today, I Will Not Be Angry

Rush hour traffic, poor customer service, and colleagues slacking off or putting the burden on you can be frustrating. For most people, one or more of these situations happens every day. There are times when bad moods and resentment can creep up on us. We lash out or harbor feelings of exasperation. Sometimes, the recipient of an outburst was not even the person that caused the anger in the first place. A bad day at work is taken out on your partner or children. It's not fair to those in your life and will only make you feel worse later. This Reiki principle focuses on letting go of this anger. Forgive the person that hurt you or made you angry. Breathe, clear your mind, and do not let anger affect your daily life.

Release your anger by acknowledging your emotions. Repeat this principle to yourself when you are agitated and take deep breaths. Write it out if you need a visual reminder. Remember that anger is an internal manifestation of emotion. External events may trigger these emotions, but your reaction is the result of internal negative energy. Think carefully about why you are angry and the events that provoked aggression. Maybe this situation has happened before. Think about how you dealt with the previous situation and whether your anger was really worthwhile. Focus your energy on letting go. An effective way to release anger is to breathe in deeply and then exhale all your negative emotions.

Just for Today, I Will Be Grateful

Being happy is not always easy. We want things that we cannot have. It is not a bad thing if you are motivated and striving for aspirational goals. But sometimes, our desires get the best of us. Bitterness ensues, and people forget about the things they have in their life. Be thankful for your comfortable home, good health, supportive family, good job that puts food on the table, and unconditional love. Being grateful establishes positivity and becomes an attractive force for happiness.

Gratitude enhances your life through feelings of content and fulfillment. Practicing gratitude is simple; all you have to do is take a closer look at what's around you. Take a moment and see the things you have in your life. There are so many objects, people, and situations that you can be thankful for. A good gratitude strategy is to write down a few things that bring you great joy. Remind yourself of those things when you feel negativity creeping into your mind.

Just for Today, I Will Do My Work Honestly

Working towards a task or goal provides fulfillment. This is an opportunity to make a difference in the world. It gives purpose to your life and allows for the achievement of goals. Sometimes, people stray from their tasks, procrastinate, or get distracted by outside factors. Identify these moments and work to refocus on the task at hand when you do. Reiki principles consider work to be a source of inspiration, so focus on your job today. Work purposefully and honestly. Give your all to the job you have to do, and you will experience a sense of belonging.

Working honestly requires conscious effort. It is an opportunity to learn, interact, and make a difference. Treat your colleagues with respect and cherish leadership relationships. The people around you will realize your positivity and look to you as a role model. Strive to do your best every day, even when it is difficult. Break your work down into manageable chunks so you can achieve something, even if it's small. Integrity is a big part of work, so ensure all your actions are impeccable. Be honest about your limitations and tell mentors when you are struggling with tasks. Accept that failure may happen, but know that you tried your best. Your job is a chance to practice every principle of Reiki, so embrace it with open arms.

Just for Today, I Will Be Kind to Every Living Thing

Kindness is one thing we could all use more of, and giving creates fulfillment, happiness and makes a difference. Kindness should not only be shown to other people but displayed to animals, the environment, and any other living thing. Sharing your content, kindness, and love will have a lasting impact on the recipient. Be a light bearer for all of humanity.

Realize when you are unkind and do your best to rectify the situation. Sometimes we are hard on ourselves, which creates discontent and breaks down your self-confidence. Forgive yourself when you are unkind and seek ways to feel better. Visit a friend, volunteer your time for a good cause, or do some gardening. Something as simple as smiling at a stranger or putting out food for a stray animal makes a big difference. Being kind is easy, so let it shine.

The five Reiki principles apply to every person for every day of their lives. These principles are a behavioral guide to make you a better person. Just for today...stop worrying, release anger, work honestly, be grateful, and be kind.

THREE

Three Pillars of Reiki

REIKI SESSIONS BENEFIT FROM MINDFULNESS. IT OPENS UP THE practitioner and recipient for intentional and meaningful healing. Mikao Usui focuses on three principles of Reiki. Each principle has a unique purpose, and one cannot exist without the other. The pillars help the practitioner to maintain spiritual hygiene, it creates a serene environment, and focuses the mind on Reiki. Putting the ego aside is another purpose of the pillars because removing the ego concentrates attention on energy channeling. These pillars also create and strengthen the connection between the patient and the practitioner. These three pillars are called Gassho, Reiji-ho, and Chiryo

Gassho

Gassho is defined as placing the palms of the hands together. The pronunciation of Gassho is "gash-show." The hands are in a prayer position at about the level of the heart. Practitioners frequently use Gassho when the Reiki treatment starts and for daily meditation. Many people think Gassho focuses on meditation, but that is not the case. Gassho ignites healing energies and sets the scene for mindfulness. Practitioners concentrate by using the tips of the middle finger as a focus point. It is all about staying in the moment, intention, and breathing. Gassho also plays a central role in the other two pillars.

Worldly problems affect people every day, even if you are a Reiki practitioner. These worries cannot be allowed to interfere with a Reiki session. Gassho helps practitioners to practice spiritual hygiene for five to ten minutes at the start of the session. It cleanses the sacred Reiki space and enables mindfulness. This mindset activates guidance and positive energies.

Some people use Gassho to prepare an energetic space through space cleansing rituals or burning herbs. This process creates an atmosphere for Reiki energy to manifest itself. The Reiki recipient then experiences energy from the first step into the Reiki space. They understand the intention of the session and open themselves to energetic forces. Most Reiki practitioners enter Gassho again when the patient is on the bed so that their intention focuses on the patient alone. They find the energy within themselves and wait for their fingers to ignite before starting the treatment.

Returning to Gassho may occur at any time during the session. Your patient is in a relaxed environment, so it will not bother them if you have a pause in the treatment. Gassho is a space of safety. It does not judge when your mind strays and enables your intuition. It gives a practitioner renewed energy, focus, and guidance on how to continue the session. Some therapists practice Gassho at the patient's head or feet and wait for a glow or sign from the recipient's body. These signs help practitioners to find areas that require energy or need further treatment.

Gassho is an opportunity to give thanks. Practitioners often stand at the feet of the patient using the Gassho position. This final Gassho is a reflection opportunity where the practitioner thanks Reiki for giving energy during the treatment. Some therapists envision a final energy stream before grounding themselves back into reality.

Reiji-Ho

Reiji-ho, pronounced "Ray-Gee-Ho," is a spiritual indication and prayer request. Reiji-ho invites guidance for the session. Usually, Reiji-ho forms part of Gassho before starting the treatment. During Reiji-ho, the practitioner asks that Reiki energy guides their hands to areas that require the most attention. A beginner Reiki practitioner usually focuses on specific hand positions.

In contrast, higher-level practitioners use Reiji-ho as an intuitive guide for hand placement. But, Reiji-ho can help practitioners to refocus their energy on hand positions when there is uncertainty about the flow. They also pray that the recipient experiences total and long-lasting healing.

During Gassho, the practitioner asks for guidance through the pillar of Reiji-ho. While in the prayer position, the practitioner senses many things. Practitioners listen to their bodies, emotions, visible cues, and reactions from the patient. Receiving divine guidance may take some time, so this process is never rushed as it sets the tone for the rest of the treatment. Some practitioners feel sensations throughout their bodies, while others hear specific instructions.

Reiji-ho requires trust. The practitioner must trust themselves, the patient, the universe, and the guiding system. The patient also needs to trust the practitioner and therapeutic interventions. Along with trust, Reiki treatment inspires mindfulness from all parties. The practitioner becomes an energy vessel, which serves a greater power and promotes goodness in the world. Reiji-ho enables therapists to receive information, trust it intuitively, and take action for maximum energy flow to the patient's most desperate areas. Sometimes, a practitioner finds themselves losing focus during a session. When this situation happens, the therapist returns to Gassho for realignment with Reiji-ho guidance.

Chiryo

Chiryo means "treatment" and is pronounced "Chi-Rye-Oh." It is concerned with the actual session and the person administering the treatment. Chiryo focuses on action, which is essential for successful healing. It focuses on removing ego from the practitioner using normal hand routines and guidance through intuition. The practitioner channels Reiki energy as it decides where the flow can be used best for the recipient. Chiryo flows change as the Reiki practitioner intuitively receives information from the patient, which directs the energy to other places in the body.

Chiryo includes all mechanics of hand placement. It is not just a basic movement but guidance through intuition and energy transfers. The hands move across the body in a certain way and according to a given set of positions. Some practitioners choose to touch the skin while others hover their hands slightly above the skin. A Reiki Master may even use other energy transfer methods. They may use only fingertip touching, apply pressure with their palms, or use the entire hand. Some practitioners are known to tap, gaze, blow, stroke, or visualize energies during the treatment session. Chiryo serves as the music for an energy dance between the universe, patient, and practitioner.

Since Chiryo is the application of Reiki, many practitioners spend a lot of time on it. This time helps the therapist focus and includes the other two pillars by default, as one does not exist without the other. Practitioners use hand positions as a basic guide. Yet, educating yourself and experimenting with different positions can be beneficial for growth as a Reiki therapist and positively affect the customer. Relaxation through guided energy is the end goal of Chiryo and provides healing for the patient. Chiryo often deepens the connection between the divine spirit, practitioner, and the recipient.

FOUR

Healing Hand Positions

REIKI TREATMENT CAN HAPPEN AT HOME. MANY HAND positions provide healing and energy realignment. Sometimes, you do not have the time to go for a Reiki session, or you may be away and need treatment. Self-treatment is possible and easy.

Self-Treatment with Reiki

Find a quiet room where you can practice Reiki. The area should be free of distractions and clutter so that energy can flow smoothly. Some people play Reiki music during their self-treatment. You can purchase Reiki or music or use free tracks available on Youtube. When you are ready, start with the hand positions. Hold each position for two to five minutes - depending on how much time you have available. Sometimes, your intuition guides you to hold a position for longer, or you might skip it entirely. That is totally fine; do what feels best for you. Close your eyes, focus on taking deep breaths throughout the session and clear your mind.

Prayer Position

Start by standing in the prayer position (Gassho). Place your hands together as you would in prayer with your palms touching. Hold your hand just under the chin.

Face

Cup both hands over your face covering your eyes. Let your fingertips touch gently. Do not apply any pressure, and do not cover your nose as you will struggle to breathe.

Crown

Rest your hands on top of your head. Your fingers can touch lightly, and your hands should come down on either side of your head. Do not shrug your shoulders.

Back of the Head

Move your hands to the back of your head. Place one hand just above the nape of the neck and your other hand slightly above. Keep your shoulders relaxed, and do not tense your arm muscles.

Chin

Place the bottom of your hands together and cup your jawline gently. Rest your chin in your hands. Focus on unclenching your jaw and relaxing the muscles in your face.

Throat and Heart

Place one hand on your throat with your thumb on one side and remaining fingers on the other side. Do not squeeze your throat or choke yourself. Just hold your throat gently. Place your other hand below your collarbone and over your heart.

Ribcage

Bend your elbows and rest your hands directly beneath the breast line. Your fingertips should touch each other over the upper rib cage. Remember to inhale and exhale deeply.

Solar Plexus (Abdomen)

Move your hands down your body and onto your stomach. Keep your hands slightly above your belly button.

Pelvic Area

Place your hands over the pelvic bones. Make sure your fingertips touch and relax your shoulders.

Shoulder Blades

Lift your arms and bend them at the elbow so your hands can rest on your shoulder blades. This position can be a bit tough if you are not flexible. You can also touch your shoulders if the position becomes uncomfortable.

Middle Back

Move your arms behind your back. Rest your hands on the middle of your back. Focus on your posture without slouching.

Lower Back

Move your hands to the lower back. Place them over the lower back and hip area. Select the position that is most comfortable for you or an area that requires extra energy.

Sacrum

Place your hands on the sacrum. This area is where your hips, back, and buttocks meet. It is the spot that often hurts when you are seated for a long time.

Feet

Sit down with your legs lying flat but slightly bent at the knee. Place your hands onto the top of each foot. If it is too difficult, then place your left hand over your left foot for a few minutes and then repeat the position with your right hand over your right foot. You can also place your hands on the soles of your feet if you can reach.

The feet end the Reiki self-treatment. Remember, you can place your hands on any area of your body that requires healing. Some people return to the prayer position at the end of the session. It allows reflection and slowly returns you to reality.

Side Effects

Reiki is a positive experience that relaxes the body and soothes the soul. But, Reiki can have side effects. Luckily, they don't last long, and many are part of your body's cleansing mechanisms.

Positive energy flows reverberate through your body during Reiki sessions. These vibrations will push negative energy from places in your body. This negative energy might be hiding in your muscles, tissues, or organs. The negative energy turns into toxins, which releases into your blood. As your blood circulates, your kidneys and liver start filtering out toxins. This cleansing process is an essential part of Reiki, but toxin release can lead to abdominal pain or headaches. You may experience muscle weakness and kidney or liver pain. Some people start sweating or become clammy, which is another way the body excretes negative energy.

Fatigue is another potential side effect of Reiki. Most people find Reiki relaxing, but others feel exhausted because their body is working to repair itself. Your body needs energy for healing, so it takes energy from other processes. Fatigue usually happens when someone else treats you because treatment becomes more intensive. Yet, you may still feel tired after self-treatment. Another side effect of professional treatment is discomfort because you need to lie still during the session. Talking is not part of Reiki either so keep that in mind. Nausea often accompanies tiredness and general weakness.

How to Help Side Effects

Reiki's side effects are easy to treat, and basic self-care can help you achieve Reiki's maximum benefits. So schedule some extra time to look after yourself. Drink a lot of water after your treatment. Water helps the body to remove toxins. Some people feel very thirsty after the end of the session, which is good. Thirst indicates the body is eliminating toxins. Keep a bottle of water with you for drinking right after practicing Reiki.

Rest after Reiki. You may want to take a power nap or even sleep for several hours. Some people rest by scheduling light activities for the rest of the day. Sleep helps your body to heal, so listen to your body's cues.

Some people do light exercise after Reiki. Basic exercise helps the body to release toxins and flushes out impurities faster, especially when you start to break a sweat. Try not to exercise if you are feeling overly tired. Stretching is an excellent alternative to a workout because it is not as intensive. Gently stretch specific parts of your body that feel stiff. Hold each stretch for a few minutes or until any remaining tension eases. Another option is going for a walk as nature also has energies that create positive forces in your body.

Negative thoughts and energy require release during and after treatment. You might find clarity about problems in your life or suddenly think about it from another perspective. Keep a journal to write down your thoughts about these situations. Make a note of how you are feeling and where you experienced negativity in your body. It will provide guidelines for where to focus during your next Reiki treatment.

FIVE

Reiki Attunements

A REIKI ATTUNEMENT IS SIMILAR TO INITIATION. DURING attunements, you experience the opening of energy channels and create deeper connections. An attunement is life-changing, establishes harmony, and develops a spiritual bond. Ultimately, you can become a Reiki vessel and access universal energy.

Attunement is a spiritual encounter to put it plainly. Every person has a different experience as their energy paths open to Reiki. Many students feel heat or light radiating from their bodies. Tingling throughout the body is another occurrence during the attunement. It is unique to each person, and these manifestations are often greater as you progress through the Reiki levels.

Some Reiki Masters require preparations before the attunement. Although preparation is not a necessity, it does create a framework and anticipation for attunement. Many students rekindle a spiritual connection or focus on the greater good in the universe. Some people do bodily cleanse by eliminating toxins from their lifestyles. They eat clean since heavily processed foods require more energy for digestion. Others stop smoking, avoid alcohol, and limit social media exposure. Exhibiting the five principles of Reiki before attunement is essential to releasing negativity.

First Degree

The first level, taught by a Reiki Master, encapsulates energy therapy based on the Usui Reiki system. It is often called Shoden and opens your Reiki energy channels. Usually, training includes a Reiki history lesson, hand positions for healing, and meditation. You will also learn the three pillars and five principles essential to practicing Reiki. Some courses teach students about the Chakras, or energy centers, and explain why they are part of the healing process. Mindfulness is another concept taught at the first level and is necessary for further training.

Energy channeling is the aim of first-degree attunement. You will align yourself to greater, universal energy. Identifying any energy blockages is important at this stage and must be cleared before continuing on your Reiki journey. The main energy channel runs from the top of your head and along the spine. This channel will open a permanent connection to Reiki energy. Students experience different energy levels before, during, and after the attunement. Some have a weaker energy connection as time passes, but Reiki energy remains in your life forever. The best way to strengthen this energetic connection is through frequent self-treatment and Reiki sessions with others.

Level one courses do not require students to have any previous experience in Reiki practices. The Reiki Master will teach you everything you need to know. Some programs are presented over a single weekend, while others prefer a program spanning several weeks. It really depends on your preferences, availability, and the depth of knowledge you wish to obtain. Some Reiki Masters provide attunement sessions through virtual meetings. After a first degree Reiki course, the recipient can self-treat and apply Reiki treatment to other people. The Reiki Master gives you the attunement and opens you to Reiki energy, an eternal and everlasting source. Most people practice self-treatment or assist friends and family for at least three months before attending second-degree attunement.

Second Degree

The second level, also called Okuden, strengthens the Reiki energy connection and introduces new knowledge. Students have to complete first-degree training before moving to the second degree. Second-degree attunement exposes the learner to three Reiki symbols. Most Reiki Masters provide four attunement sessions for each symbol. However, the busy nature of many people resulted in many Reiki Masters, only providing one attunement. A single attunement per symbol already creates energy pathways, but more sessions create a deeper energetic connection. A person completing the second level usually gets the title of a Reiki practitioner.

Each symbol has unique properties and strengthens your Reiki energy. The first symbol reflects power, which protects and improves healing energy. The second symbol is harmony, which represents emotional or mental balance. Finally, the distance symbol enables Reiki practitioners to heal through time and space. The symbols are explained in greater detail in a later chapter. Understanding these symbols widens the primary energy channel and enhances your capabilities.

After second degree training, students have more of a significant healing potential. Energy is used for protection and healing, while mental clarity and resilience improve substantially. Additionally, you can heal many mental conditions that others experience. Successful second-degree training enables you to send energy without being in the physical presence of the recipient. Reiki practitioners frequently use intuitive guidance when treating patients and do not only use traditional hand positions. They pick up on energy blockages and customize hand placement for the best healing treatment.

Third Degree

The highest attunement establishes a trainee as a Reiki Master. This level is known as Shinpiden. It focuses on establishing deep personal connections with spirituality and finding your inner calling. Very few people continue their training to this level as it is intense and not suited for everybody. Usually, Reiki practitioners spend a long time practicing Reiki between the second and third levels.

In third-degree attunement, practitioners increase their energy capacity. They understand that they are masters of their own destiny and can positively affect the world by living true to the Reiki principles. Reiki Masters understand their role in the broader picture and manifest their talents within a higher power. They focus not only on their own emotional and physical connection to Reiki but also use it as a method for sending energy to other people and across time.

Reiki Masters receive an attunement to other symbols. The master symbol indicates the road to enlightenment and internal power. Some Reiki Masters also receive the completion symbol that provides energetic intention and a grounding force with the Reiki energy stream. Other symbols may be taught during level three attunement. Reiki Masters fully understand the usage of these symbols and can apply them to complex situations.

Energy generation, maintenance, and sharing are part of level three. Third-degree attunement requires frequent meditation and other energy building exercises. Mindfulness, conscious decision-making, and harnessing power for the greater good is central to Reiki Masters. By the end of this level, students can share their knowledge as proficient Reiki Masters. They can also start their own training practice where they do attunements for new Reiki enthusiasts.

SIX

Reiki and the Seven Chakras
_____

THERE ARE SEVEN CHAKRAS THROUGHOUT THE BODY THAT look like wheels. Each chakra has a different activity level, which varies as situations change. In an ideal scenario, every chakra is open with heightened activity levels. But, in reality, that is not always the case. Some chakras are more active because other chakras are closed or underperforming. Opening all chakras achieves a balance between mind and instinct. Reiki can help you achieve this balance.

Seven Centers of Energy

The chakras form a straight line in the body, which creates the energy centers. Chakras located higher in the body correspond with mentality. Lower lying chakras deal with our instincts.

Root Chakra

The root chakra is also called the base chakra. It is found at the bottom of your spine. The color red represents this energy vortex. An open root chakra addresses survival and security concerns. It helps you remain grounded, assists in self-preservation, and creates physical energy. Your root chakra creates mindfulness, trust, and stability. An underactive root chakra creates nervous tension or fear. Feelings of unwelcomeness abound, and you may find yourself looking for security in status or material objects.

Sacral Chakra

The location of the sacral chakra lies between the hips and associates with the color orange. This chakra makes you expressive and governs sexuality. An open sacral chakra helps with free expression in a balanced way. It creates passion and opens you to deeper intimacy. People with a closed sacral chakra are described as being cold with no emotion, are considered unapproachable, and like to hide behind a poker face. If you feel overly emotional and increasingly sensitive, then you might have an overactive sacral chakra.

Solar Plexus Chakra

Located just above the belly button, the solar plexus chakra is also known as the navel or stomach chakra. Associated with the color yellow, control, and power are the main features of the stomach chakra. An open solar plexus chakra creates assertiveness, self-esteem, and feelings of having control. Indecisiveness and timidity are signs of a closed stomach chakra. While aggression and domination indicate an overactive chakra.

Heart Chakra

The heart chakra is close to your heart and in the middle of your chest. Green is the color of this energy center. It is no surprise that the heart chakra regulates love. This energy center helps you in relationships and makes you compassionate. It helps focus on spirituality and being conscious of group concerns. An open heart chakra fosters harmony, friendliness, and compassion. A closed chakra creates distance in relationships, and you might have a cold demeanor. Overbearing love or selfish love indicates your heart chakra is overactive.

Throat Chakra

The throat chakra uses a light, bright blue color and sits in the area of your Adam's apple. Communication is the main focus of this chakra. Talking and creative self-expression occur with a balanced throat chakra. Shyness, introversion, and staying quiet are signs of a closed throat chakra. This situation often happens when people lie. Speaking over others, talking excessively, and always curving conversations towards yourself are signs of an overactive throat chakra, which means you are distancing people by not listening.

Third-Eye Chakra

A dark blue chakra exists between your eyebrows. This position creates an image of a third eye. Clairvoyance is the main issue of this chakra. It is responsible for light, intuition, spiritual energy, and psychic abilities. An open third-eye chakra gives excellent intuition and insight. A closed chakra makes you confused, indecisive. You are likely to question your gut feelings more and often select an option chosen by someone else. Hallucinations and creating fantasies are indicators of an overactive third-eye chakra.

Crown Chakra

The final chakra is on top of your head in the area where a crown would sit. Purple is the color for this chakra, which controls spiritual wisdom. Proactive thoughts, a sense of self, and enlightenment come from a balanced crown chakra. You become aware of your actions and their effect on the world, making you change prejudicial actions. A closed crown chakra manifests in poor spiritual awareness and rigid thinking. Ignoring your own needs, spiritual addiction, and overthinking are signs of an overactive chakra.

The Chakras and the Physical Body

A chakra is part of a person's consciousness. Chakras cannot be seen with the naked eye, but they exist within your body. Each chakra connects to a specific part of the body. The healing hand positions correspond to energy centers. This connection explains why you can heal a particular area of the body with certain hand positions. The endocrine glands and the plexus that consist of bundled nerve endings interact with the chakras.

Each chakra is responsible for specific activities in the body. Symptoms in certain areas indicate the chakra is experiencing an imbalance. Explaining symptoms or issues to a Reiki healer can help them focus their energy on those parts of the body.

The root chakra provides energy to your back, spine, hips, legs, and feet. Auto-immune diseases, eating disorders, tiredness, kidney problems, and certain spinal injuries indicate a root chakra imbalance. Organs in the lower body, such as the bowel, bladder, and reproductive organs, all get energy from the sacral chakra. Indicators of an imbalance in this chakra manifest in cancer of the reproductive organs, pelvic disease, and kidney or bladder problems. The solar plexus chakra protects your upper spine, back, and abdomen. An energy imbalance in the solar plexus chakra often shows up in digestive issues and diabetes.

Circulation, blood, the heart, and lungs fall under the care of the heart chakra. Heart problems, high blood pressure, circulatory issues, and cancer are signs of an imbalance in your heart chakra. The throat chakra protects your jaw, mouth, tongue, thyroid, and throat. Problems indicating a throat chakra imbalance include thyroid issues, neck stiffness, jaw alignment, vocal issues, and asthma. The third-eye chakra is responsible for the skull, brain, nervous system, eyes, pineal, and pituitary glands. Headaches, facial issues, glaucoma, and problems with the central nervous system link to an imbalance in the third-eye chakra. The crown chakra is responsible for your brain stem, nerves, and spinal cord. Epilepsy, pain, and exhaustion are associated with a crown chakra imbalance.

Endocrine System and the Chakras

The endocrine system is a control center for the body that consists of ductless glands that transport chemicals through hormone production. Certain organs then release these hormones into your bloodstream. This process can prevent or encourage specific functions in the body. The endocrine system adjusts the level of hormones, so you have maximum health.

Endocrine glands correspond with the chakras. Each chakra position aligns with the gland's locations in the body. Chakras and glands have a holistic bond and function as one. There is an undeniable connection between the physical functions of the body and mental or emotional health. Daily activities like exercise, eating healthy, and getting enough sleep are just as important as mental stimulation and emotional stability.

A chakra imbalance affects a specific part of your

endocrine system. The affected glands cannot function optimally, and you become sick from this imbalance. The glands include the adrenal cortex for survival, ovaries for development, pancreas for metabolism, thymus for digestion, thyroid for immunity, pituitary gland for growth, and the pineal gland for body rhythm. Reiki energy can help people find their balance by activating the chakras and tapping into the universal energy source.

SEVEN

Reiki and Meditation

MEDITATION IS A COMPANION FOR REIKI HEALING. REIKI
students, healers, and patients often find meditation beneficial.
Meditation is a method that focuses on a person's awareness
and attention so that they achieve a clear mind and become
emotionally stable. Stress, mental fatigue, and unhappiness
cause overwhelming emotions. Sometimes, you just need a
break from it all, and meditation can help you process these
feelings. Meditation is a great way to recharge. It's good to
frequently practice regardless of very specific positive or negative emotions existing. The goal of Reiki meditation is a focus
on intention and mental clarity.

Cleansing Meditation

A cleansing meditation can help you release negative energy.
Find a quiet area and sit in a comfortable position or lie down
flat. Breathe in deeply and start to relax your body. Focus on
positive energy entering your body as you inhale. Pay attention to happiness flowing through your body. Next, breathe
out slowly and feel your body releasing stress and any
lingering negative energy. Imagine all of these negative feel-

ings leaving your body and making space for positivity. Repeat this breathing exercise five to ten times. You can repeat this process as much as you'd like or until you feel your positive energy increasing. Many people do cleansing meditation at the start of longer meditative practices. It puts them in the right frame of mind to focus on Reiki energy.

Mantra Meditation

The five principles we discussed earlier are a great starting point for meditation. Choose one of the principles that you feel you need to work on and focus on that. Pay attention to your breathing while you think about this principle mantra. Some people prefer to say the mantra out loud, which helps your thoughts not stray. Remember, the principles focus on not worrying, not being angry, being grateful, doing your work honestly, and being kind. If you are new to meditation, you could choose one mantra to use during your meditation.

Reiki Zen Meditation

Zen meditation focuses on paying attention to what's happening on the inside. It is slightly different from Reiki, but the system remains the same. Reiki adds internal energy and intention to the meditative practice. Most importantly, you first need to find a quiet place to meditate. The area you choose should be free from distractions, technology, and outside noise.

You can sit or lie down during Reiki Zen meditation - choose the most comfortable position for you. Close your eyes. Breathe normally while letting your thoughts run free. Now focus on clearing your mind and creating a neutral mental canvas. Use your nose to inhale and mouth to exhale. Pay attention to your lungs, expanding as you breathe in and becoming flat as you breathe out. After about ten breaths, focus your attention internally. Pay attention to energy movement inside your body. Feel the energy flowing into your body with every inhale. Focus on it filling your mind, head, throat, chest, abdomen, arms, legs, spine, hips, legs, and feet. Pay attention to the energy in every part of your body. Focus on energy in each part of your body as long as necessary before moving to the next part. Once you are done, take a few deep breaths. Open your eyes, and you will notice you are leaving your quiet area feeling different than before.

Color or Energy Meditation

Chakra meditation is another option that accompanies Reiki. This type of meditation focuses on color and energy. Each chakra is an energy vortex, and paying attention to it can help you channel energy to that area. This focus assists in healing and opening the chakras. Some people only focus on one chakra during this meditation, while others prefer going through all the energy centers.

Find a quiet space like a secluded garden or quiet room in your house to sit comfortably. Close your eyes here. Start the meditation by breathing normally. After a few breaths, visualize a chakra color. Focus on its appearance in your subconscious and see the swirling energy in your mind. Visualize the color getting darker then lighter. Keep your breathing steady. You can inhale deeper at this point and hold your breath for a few counts before exhaling slowly. Imagine you are inhaling the chakra color and associated energy. Feel it filling all the voids in your body, especially the body parts associated with that color. Repeat this process several times.

Focusing on an energy vortex in a specific part of the body is another option. Bring the chakra positions to mind and focus all your attention on that part of the body. For example, you can focus on the third-eye chakra. Visualize a dark blue energy vortex between your eyebrows. Focus on the swirls and channel energy into that area. If you want to do a full-body color meditation, then start with the first chakra (root chakra) located at the bottom of your spine and move up the chakras from that point.

Center Finger Focus

Our busy lives and stress often distract us during meditation, and you will need something to help maintain focus. The Center Finger Technique is not a meditation in itself. Instead, it allows you to pay more attention throughout your meditation.

Place yourself in the Gassho position. This prayer position requires your hands together under your chin. With your palms facing each other, place each finger from the left hand against its corresponding finger on the right hand. Focus specifically on your middle finger placement. Your middle finger is the center finger. Now, close your eyes and focus on the center fingers during your meditation. Continue inhaling deeply and exhaling slowly. Focus on your middle fingers as soon as you catch your thoughts drifting. Place light pressure onto your middle fingers if you need additional guidance.

The Center Finger Technique is suitable for all types of meditation. You can also use it alone to tune your mind into Reiki. Some people use it to create focus before starting another form of meditation. The prayer position frequently becomes the main position a person uses throughout their meditation because it is comfortable sitting or lying down.

Some people play music to accompany Reiki meditation. Reiki music is unique because it exudes specific frequencies that interact with each energy. These frequencies frequently assist in healing and will help you relax. Other people choose to burn herbs before or throughout their meditation. Herbs are a natural cure for many ailments, and smelling them can improve a person's health. Some people have a special pillow they sit on, a set meditation time every day, or prefer to wear certain clothes, making them more comfortable. Meditation is a personal practice, so you have to find the things that work for you.

Meditation is a cornerstone of Reiki. People who receive Reiki treatments often enter a meditative state during treatment because they are working to clear their minds and breathe deeply. On the other hand, meditation forms part of attunements, so all Reiki students must make meditation part of their lives. Reiki Masters meditate daily to channel their Reiki energy and connect them to the universal energy source. The most important thing is to make time for your Reiki meditation, just like you prioritize time for other activities. Adding meditation to your schedule helps you cope with life's daily challenges, emphasizes the five Reiki principles, and opens your chakras for healing.

EIGHT

Manifest Your Goals with Reiki Symbols

REIKI IS A POWERFUL TOOL IN YOUR HEALTH AND WELLNESS arsenal, and it can also help you achieve your goals. During Reiki attunement, you will be taught five symbols. A Reiki Master introduces the first three symbols during the second-degree attunement and the last two in third-degree attunement. There are other symbols in Reiki, but these five symbols are the basis for manifestation.

Reiki Symbols

Reiki symbols accompany the healing hands' positions and meditation. The symbols create an energy concentration and focus power in specific areas. They provide balance, harmony and open a person to healing. Symbols assist your emotions and mentality. It allows you to surround yourself with energy, which enables energy creation inside your body. Symbols align chakras, and each chakra also has a symbol. Here we will cover the five main symbols you need to know to start.

The Power Symbol

The power symbol, also known as Cho Ku Rei, or Bright Shining Light, resembles a music note with a spiral tail. It helps in manifesting energy, increases protections, and accelerates the healing process. The power symbol increases your potential immediately, so practitioners often use it at the start or end of treatment. It looks like a coil and funnels intense power but blocks all negative energies exuded by the patient.

Mental and Emotional Healing Symbol

Sei Hei Ki is an emotional and mental symbol with a focus on balance. This symbol helps to heal emotions, strengthen mental capacity, and balance emotions. The symbol is often called the harmony symbol since it aligns the body and mind. It helps release intense negative emotions, improve memory when drawn above the head, and is frequently used by Reiki Masters during challenging times.

The Distance Symbol

The distance symbol is known as Hon Sha Ze Sho Nen or the connection symbol. It focuses on bridging the barriers between time and distance. Using this symbol establishes a spiritual connection and enables distant healing. The distance symbol transcends across time constraints described as the past, present, and future. This energy has access to all people and can affect future events.

The Master Symbol

The Dai Ko Myo, or master symbol, is given in third-degree attunement. It provides enlightenment and empowers healing of the soul. Reiki Masters use this symbol, along with the previous three, to generate tremendous power. The master symbol encapsulates all the Reiki beliefs and focuses on any form of healing.

The Completion Symbol

The completion symbol is known as Raku. It grounds a Reiki Master and aligns the chakras. Only used during attunement, it secures Reiki energy into the body and ignites the chakras. The symbol looks similar to a lightning bolt, which reminds the Reiki Masters of their connection to life force energy.

The Manifestation Path

Some people always seem to get everything they want in life, while others struggle to achieve their dreams. The first person uses manifestation while the second person has learned to leave things up to chance. Manifestation is the process of realizing your goals by using the power of your mind, beliefs, and feelings to make them real. Reiki is a great way to manifest your goals since it implements more intention and focuses on specific aspects of life. The symbols can also help in reaching your goals as they help with energy processing and intention.

Reiki is for the benefit of all. It promotes goodness and balance. Reiki energy only appeals to intentions that are for the greater good of a person. So, construct goals or dreams that are beneficial to you but will not harm others. You cannot manifest a goal and find success if that idea hurts another person to create negative energy. It is impossible because Reiki energy only works as a positive and actively works to replace negativity. Think about your goals and ensure that they are not for selfish reasons.

The path of manifestation is specific. First, you have to think about what you want to achieve. Ideas start manifesting in the causal plane and move to the mental plane when you start fleshing out the details of what you want. Think about what you are seeking. For example, think about how much weight you want to lose (a specific number) rather than just saying you want to lose weight. Write down your thoughts in great detail as if you have already achieved your goal. So the example would eventually morph into "I have lost x pounds." This type of intention convinces you and the universe that manifestation is possible. Next, send Reiki energy to this conviction. This energy moves your goal from the mental plane to the astral plane, where emotions manifest itself. Continuous positive energy and belief transfer the goal from the astral plane to the physical plane where the final manifestation takes place.

Reiki energy helps in manifesting your goals. Lay your hands on the paper daily for 10 to 15 minutes and send Reiki energy to your goal. Practitioners can draw the Reiki symbols on this paper to focus more energy on the goal. Another option is to draw or visualize the symbols in the air or above your paper during the Reiki session. Start with the distance symbol as the energy needs to move across time and into the future. Next, move on to the mental and emotional healing symbol as it helps to transfer energy into the astral plane. Finally, apply the power symbol for great strength in achieving your goals.

Reiki meditation is another method that assists in manifestation. Find a quiet spot and start with the Gassho position. Inhale and exhale deeply while focusing on your goal. Say your goal aloud to the universe or focus on it in your mind. Be clear in what you want and repeat your goal several times, similar to a mantra. Imagine yourself achieving the goal and optimistic feelings of success. Now, focus your attention on the Reiki symbols surrounding your visualized goal. Draw them in your mind one-by-one. You can also use your hands to draw the symbols in the air in front of you. Pay attention to the energy emitted from each of the symbols and their interaction with your goal. Once you find inner peace from the imagery, release your goal to the universe. See it float away, surrounded by the Reiki symbols.

Achieving your goal now rests with the universal Reiki energy. Do not worry about it further. Meditate and use the symbols every day to manifest your goals. Continuously send Reiki energy to your goals. Remember that you can also send Reiki energy to another person's goals. Always share your power with your daily and friends in a truly unselfish way. Feel excited about the good things to come while being thankful for everything you already possess in your life.

Conclusion

Reiki taps into a life force energy present throughout the universe and touches each person, whether they be a believer or skeptic. Reiki is a healing practice that includes meditation, symbols, and intention. It offers many benefits to recipients, practitioners, and Masters. Reiki restores emotional balance and creates alignment between the mind and physical body. It reduces stress and tension, cleanses a person from negative energy, and enhances positive energy flow. Reiki often complements traditional healthcare treatments as it calms patients and increases healing.

Reiki has five principles that become mantras for all people practicing Reiki. Just for today, I will not worry. Just for today, I will not be angry. Just for today, I will be grateful. Just for today, I will do my work honestly. Just for today, I will be kind to every living thing. Repeat these principles for a purposeful life.

The three pillars are the cornerstone of Reiki. Gassho, Reiji-Ho, and Chiryo are present in all parts of Reiki. Which focuses the mind on healing and energy with a prayer request that guides the practitioner's intuition during treatment with the placing of hands in healing positions.

Studying Reiki requires attunements that open students to the energy that can heal themselves and others. During first degree attunement, students learn the Reiki basics for treating themselves and others. Second-degree attunement strengthens energy channels and activates the power, harmony, and distance symbols. The final degree focuses on becoming one with the world and attunes students to the Master symbols. Higher Reiki degrees attune a person to energy, strengthens energetic channels, and provides new healing ways.

Reiki energy manifests in the body through seven chakras. Each chakra is a ball of energy in a straight line from the spine's base to the head's top. Each color corresponds to a specific chakra, which helps create greater focus during meditation. The chakras and endocrine system communicate with each other to produce healing properties within the body. Each chakra energizes and heals the body's represented parts, which stabilizes emotions and mental health.

Meditation and symbolism play a vital role in Reiki. Meditation is a relaxing and powerful practice that supports mindfulness. It creates clarity of mind and enables the manifestation of goals. Reiki is a wholesome energy belief system that works through meditation, healing, and powerful symbols. Tap into your universal energy stream and see how you can make a difference in someone else's life. Good luck!

References

Bedosky, L. (2020). All about Reiki: How this type of energy healing works, and its health benefits. Everyday Health. https://www.everydayhealth.com/reiki/

Cleveland Clinic. (2019). Reiki self-treatment: Procedure details. https://my.clevelandclinic.org/health/treatments/21080-reiki-self-treatment/procedure-details

Crook, G. (n.d.). Levels of Reiki. Reiki World. http://www.reikiworld.net/Reiki/Levels_of_Reiki.htm

Desy, P. I. (2019). Basic Reiki hand placements for self treatment. Learn Religions. https://www.learnreligions.com/reiki-hand-placements-for-self-treatment-1731723

Frazier, K. (2018). Engaging in the flow of Reiki through its three pillars. Author Karen Frazier. https://www.authorkarenfrazier.com/blog/engaging-in-the-flow-of-reiki-through-its-three-pillars#/

Gibson, C. J. (2018). Meditation with Reiki can help reduce your stress. Medium. https://medium.com/thrive-global/what-is-reiki-how-this-practice-could-help-your-meditation-60e4b0583f78

Herbert, C. (2017). How Reiki symbols can change your

life. Gaia. https://www.gaia.com/article/reiki-symbols-to-change-your-life

Mental Health & Performance Inc. (n.d.). 8 Benefits of Reiki healing. Mindset First. https://mindsetfirst.ca/8-benefits-of-reiki-healing/

Mindvalley. (2018). Reiki meditation: Shut out the chaos and master inner peace. https://blog.mindvalley.com/reiki-meditation/

Nunez, K. (2020a). How to use Reiki principles to boost well-being. Health Line. https://www.healthline.com/health/reiki-principles

Nunez, K. (2020b). Does Reiki have side effects or risks? Health Line. https://www.healthline.com/health/disadvantages-of-reiki

Pope, T. (n.d.). Chakras and the endocrine system. Timothy Pope. https://www.timothypope.co.uk/chakras-endocrine-system/

Reiki Light. (n.d.). The three degrees of Reiki. https://reiki-light.co.uk/the-three-degrees-of-reiki/

Reiki Universe. (2014). Manifesting goals with Reiki. https://reikuniverse.tumblr.com/post/77372355736/manifesting-goals-with-reiki

Ronquillo, H. (2014). 5 Reiki principles to promote a healthy, loving life. Mind Body Green. https://www.mindbodygreen.com/0-15751/5-reiki-principles-to-promote-a-healthy-loving-life.html

The International Center for Reiki Training. (n.d.). What is Reiki? https://www.reiki.org/faqs/what-reiki

Vlad. (n.d.). 24 Reiki symbols and how to use them in Usui, Karuna, and Shamballa. ReikiScoop. https://reikiscoop.com/reiki-symbols-and-their-meaning-from-usui-to-karuna-and-shamballa/

WellnessWrx. (n.d.). 5 Easy self-care tips you need after every Reiki treatment. https://wellnesswrx.ca/5-easy-self-care-tips-you-need-after-every-reiki-treatment/

About the Author

Monique Joiner Siedlak is a writer, witch, and warrior on a mission to awaken people to their greatest potential through the power of storytelling infused with mysticism, modern paganism, and new age spirituality. At the young age of 12, she began rigorously studying the fascinating philosophy of Wicca. By the time she was 20, she was self-initiated into the craft, and hasn't looked back ever since. To this day, she has authored over 40 books pertaining to the magick and mysteries of life.

To find out more about Monique Joiner Siedlak artistically, spiritually, and personally, feel free to visit her **official website**.

www.mojosiedlak.com

facebook.com/mojosiedlak

twitter.com/mojosiedlak

instagram.com/mojosiedlak

pinterest.com/mojosiedlak

bookbub.com/authors/monique-joiner-siedlak

More Books by Author

Practical Magick
Wiccan Basics
Candle Magick
Wiccan Spells
Love Spells
Abundance Spells
Herb Magick
Moon Magick
Creating Your Own Spells
Gypsy Magic
Protection Magick
Celtic Magick
Shamanic Magick

African Magic
Hoodoo
Seven African Powers: The Orishas
Cooking for the Orishas
Lucumi: The Ways of Santeria
Voodoo of Louisiana
Haitian Vodou

Orishas of Trinidad
Connecting with your Ancestors

The Yoga Collective
Yoga for Beginners
Yoga for Stress
Yoga for Back Pain
Yoga for Weight Loss
Yoga for Flexibility
Yoga for Advanced Beginners
Yoga for Fitness
Yoga for Runners
Yoga for Energy
Yoga for Your Sex Life
Yoga to Beat Depression and Anxiety
Yoga for Menstruation
Yoga to Detox Your Body
Yoga to Tone Your Body

A Natural Beautiful You
Creating Your Own Body Butter
Creating Your Own Body Scrub
Creating Your Own Body Spray

Last Chance
Join My Newsletter!

If you missed it, I have a free gift available for you and wanted to remind you it's still available.

mojosiedlak.com/self-help-and-yoga-newsletter

Thank you for reading my book.
I really appreciate all your feedback and would love to hear what you have to say! Please leave your review at your favorite retailer!